JAN - - '04

CHINESE NEW YEAR

Written by Alice K. Flanagan

Illustrated by Svetlana Zhurkina

Content Advisers: Jennifer Lo and Li-Chun Chen, Chinese American Association of Minnesota, Minneapolis, Minnesota

Reading Adviser: Dr. Linda D. Labbo, Department of Reading Education, College of Education, The University of Georgia

COMPASS POINT BOOKS

MINNEAPOLIS, MINNESOTA

Compass Point Books
3109 West 50th Street, #115
Minneapolis, MN 55410

Visit Compass Point Books on the Internet at *www.compasspointbooks.com*
or e-mail your request to *custserv@compasspointbooks.com*

Editors: E. Russell Primm, Emily J. Dolbear, and Patricia Stockland
Designer: The Design Lab

Library of Congress Cataloging-in-Publication Data
Flanagan, Alice K.
   Chinese New Year / written by Alice K. Flanagan ; illustrated by Svetlana Zhurkina ;
reading adviser, Linda D. Labbo.
       p. cm. — (Holidays and festivals)
 Includes bibliographical references and index.
   ISBN 0-7565-0479-1 (alk. paper)
  1. Chinese New Year—Juvenile literature. 2. Chinese New Year—United States—Juvenile literature.
3. China—Social life and customs—Juvenile literature. I. Zhurkina, Svetlana. II. Labbo, Linda D.
III. Title. IV. Series: Holidays and festivals (Compass Point Books)
   GT4905.F53 2004
   394.261—dc21   2002155740

Table of Contents

NOTE: In this book, words that are defined in the glossary are in **bold** the first time they appear in the text.

Follow a dancing dragon down the street. Listen to firecrackers pop, and eat sweet treats.

You can do all of these things during Chinese New Year. The holiday is **celebrated** in Chinese communities all over the world. It lasts for fifteen days.

People celebrate Chinese New Year in late winter or early spring with wishes of good luck, health, and happiness. The holiday begins on the first day of a full moon between January 20 and February 20. The Chinese **lunar calendar** shows this different date every year.

How Did Chinese New Year Begin?

People have been celebrating Chinese New Year for more than four thousand years. Farmers started the holiday in China to mark the end of winter and the beginning of spring. As soon as winter was over, farmers worked hard to get the land ready for spring planting. They cleaned up the fields and planted new seeds. Then they prayed for a good harvest of crops.

Chinese farmers thought of spring as the start of a New Year. They cleaned their homes and held a feast to celebrate a new beginning. Then they rested until they had to work in the fields again.

The Story of a Wild Beast

How did dragons, lions, lights, and firecrackers become part of the farmers' celebration? People say that it all started one winter long ago when a wild beast attacked one of the villages. At first, everyone was afraid of the beast. Then they discovered what the beast feared: It did not like loud noises, the color red, or bright lights. To keep the beast away from their homes, people painted the doors of their houses red. They built fires and set off firecrackers until the beast ran away from their village. Today, wild beasts (also known as Nian, or Year Monster), bright lights, firecrackers, and the color red are still important parts of the New Year celebration.

Getting Ready for the New Year

Chinese families spend many days getting ready for the New Year. They begin by cleaning their houses. Everyone helps sweep all the dirt out the door, along with the bad luck that is hiding in the house. People believe that if the house is not clean, there will be no room for all of the good things the New Year will bring. Some people even go to the cemetery to clean the stones that mark the place where their loved ones are buried.

When the house is clean, family members decorate it. They hang up red and gold banners called **scrolls.** On the scrolls they write good wishes for the family in the coming year. Then they put out plants and flowers that will bring them good luck. Some people believe if flower buds open on New Year's Day, then they will have a year of good luck.

Many families keep a kumquat tree in the house for good luck in the coming year. Its fruit looks like a tiny orange. Other families decorate their houses with branches from peach and plum trees. The Chinese believe that peach and plum flowers bring long life.

Many Chinese families shop for new clothes to wear in the New Year. Much of the clothing they buy is red, which stands for happiness. Often, they get their hair cut. Some people put lime leaves in their bath water before they bathe. They believe lime leaves will make them extra clean.

Everybody tries to pay bills before the New Year. They also try to stop fighting and forgive those who have hurt them.

Saying Good-bye to the Old Year

After everyone in the family cleans the house and decorates it, they say good-bye to Tsun Kwan, the Kitchen God. The Chinese believe that the Kitchen God watches their actions throughout the year. On the last night of the old year, he leaves Earth to visit the Jade Emperor in heaven. There the gods talk about how family members have treated one another during the year.

To honor the Kitchen God, families prepare a special dinner. They put out sweet foods for him to take on his trip. They pray that he will say only "sweet things" about them to the Jade Emperor. Then, to send the Kitchen God to heaven, they burn his picture and set off firecrackers outside the house to ward off evil spirits. They are hopeful that the Kitchen God will return on the first day of the New Year to bring them good luck.

The New Year's Eve Feast

Families also have a feast on the last night of the old year. This night is called New Year's Eve. Before the feast, families seal the doors of their homes with strips of red paper to keep out bad spirits. They decorate the doors with "lucky phrases" written on paper in gold ink. Then the whole family gathers for dinner. If someone cannot be there, a place is set for that person along with an empty chair.

There are many different kinds of food served at dinner. Often, fish, chicken, pork, and beef are served with vegetables and noodles.

Usually these dinners are held in the home. Today, however, more and more Chinese Americans are going to restaurants.

Many Chinese people stay awake all night on New Year's Eve to make sure that everyone is safe from Nian, the wild beast. Then, on New Year's morning, they celebrate their good luck. They are lucky to have survived and not have been eaten by the beast.

Happy
New Year's Day!

On New Year's Day, families break the seals on their doors. They open the doors to let in good luck. Throughout the day, everyone tries to show good manners. There are no bad words spoken. People believe that whatever happens on this day will show what kind of luck they can expect in the coming year.

On this first day of the New Year, people visit family and then see friends. Visitors bring special gifts like flowers, fruit, melon seeds, and New Year's cakes. Each gift brings with it a special wish for the coming year. Oranges stand for money and wealth. Tangerines stand for good luck. New Year's cakes and candies stand for peace and togetherness.

Adults give children red envelopes called Lai-See on New Year's Day. They write the family name or a good-luck message on the envelope in gold ink. Good-luck money is placed inside the envelope. Only paper money is given because coins are thought to bring bad luck.

The Lantern Festival and Golden Dragon Parade

A three-day Lantern Festival ends the Chinese New Year celebration in China. During the **festival,** people hang **lanterns** in the streets and light fire-crackers to scare away evil spirits. The lanterns are made of paper, glass, or **silk.** They are cut in the shape of birds, fish, stars, and flowers. In the United States, the holiday ends with a Golden Dragon Parade.

In many Chinese communities, people line the streets to watch parades. Drums and horns announce the **floats** and the dancing dragon. The dragon is made of paper or silk stretched over **bamboo** poles. Sometimes it can be 50 feet (15 meters) long! Twelve to fifty dancers carry the poles. They twist and turn the dragon's body and make its huge eyes blink. Popping firecrackers bring the New Year's celebration to an end.

Things You Might See During Chinese New Year

The Tray of Togetherness (Chuen-Hop)

To welcome visitors to their homes, many families put out a food tray. There are eight parts in the tray. Each part has a special food in it. Some people believe that if you eat the lotus seeds, you will have sons. If you eat the melon, you will grow tall and have good health. If you eat the coconut, your family will stay together. If you eat the watermelon seeds, you will have plenty of whatever you need.

The Family Altar

On New Year's Eve or New Year's Day, families use a low table to set up an altar in their house. They place things that have special meaning to them on the altar. These objects include pictures of loved ones who have died. Families also place bowls of fruit on the altar to bring good luck in the coming year. On the wall behind the table, they hang red and gold banners with New Year wishes for wealth, good luck, and happiness.

The Chinese Calendar

The Chinese New Year is based on the Chinese calendar. It is different from the calendar used in the United States. Each year of the Chinese calendar is named after one of twelve animals. The animals are the rat, the ox, the tiger, the rabbit, the dragon, the snake, the horse, the sheep (or goat), the monkey, the rooster, the dog, and the pig. After twelve years, the animals repeat in the same order again.

The Chinese believe you share some **traits** with the animal that rules the year in which you were born. The rat is friendly and busy. The ox is loyal and dependable. The tiger is brave and quick to act. The rabbit is shy and quiet. The dragon is strong and wise. The snake is tricky and cautious. The horse is cheerful and free-spirited. The sheep is trustworthy and loving. The monkey is funny and mischievous. The rooster is proud and hardworking. The dog is loyal and faithful. The pig is smart and kind.

A Dragon

A dragon has special meaning for the Chinese. It stands for strength and good luck. Every Chinese New Year's parade ends with a dragon made of bamboo poles and paper or silk. The Chinese dragon is strong because it is made up of the parts of many animals. It has the eyes of a rabbit, the mouth of a camel, the horns of a deer, the scales of a **carp,** the whiskers of a catfish, the claws of a hawk, the legs of a tiger, the ears of an ox, and the body of a snake.

28

What You Can Do During Chinese New Year

Chinese New Year is a holiday that celebrates the importance of family and friends. Preparing for the New Year and a new start in life is just as important as celebrating the first day of the New Year and the parades that follow. You can do many things to enjoy the New Year. Here are some ideas:

* Make banners with good-luck wishes and poems on them. Give them to your teachers, neighbors, and friends.
* Visit your grandparents and aunts and uncles. Take them a lucky banner you have made.
* Take flowers or fruit to family members and friends.
* Clean your room and help clean the house.

Glossary

bamboo a tropical plant with woody, hollow stems used to make furniture and other things

carp a large fish whose scales are said to make up part of the Chinese dragon

celebrated had a party or honored a special event

festival a holiday or celebration

floats platforms on wheels that carry displays or exhibits in a parade

lanterns types of lights or lamps

lunar calendar a calendar that uses the moon to decide days, weeks, months, and years

scrolls rolls of parchment or paper, usually with writing on them

seals things that close or fasten tightly

silk cloth made from the fine, soft fiber spun by silkworms

trait a feature or quality about something that makes it different from others

Where You Can Learn More About Chinese New Year

At the Library

Bouchard, David, and Zhong-Yang Huang. *The Dragon New Year: A Chinese Legend.* Atlanta: Peachtree Publishers, 1999.

Hoyt-Goldsmith, Diane, and Lawrence Migdale. *Celebrating Chinese New Year.* New York: Holiday House, Inc., 1999.

Marx, David F. *Chinese New Year.* New York: Scholastic Library, 2002.

Robinson, Fay. *Chinese New Year–A Time for Parades, Family, and Friends.* Berkeley Heights, N.J.: Enslow Publishers, 2001.

On the Web

Chinese Culture Center of San Francisco
http://www.c-c-c.org/chineseculture/zodiac/zodiac.html
For a description of each of the animals in the Chinese calendar

FamilyCulture.com
http://www.familyculture.com/Chinese_new_year.htm
For a detailed description of the holiday

Through the Mail

Chinese Historical Society of America
965 Clay Street
San Francisco, CA 94108
For information about the culture, history, and contributions of Chinese Americans

On the Road

Chinese Culture Center of San Francisco
750 Kearny Street, 3rd Floor
San Francisco, CA 94108
415/986-1822
To view exhibits of Chinese American art, history, and culture

Index

About the Author and Illustrator

Alice K. Flanagan writes books for children and teachers. Since she was a young girl, she has enjoyed writing. She has written more than seventy books. Some of her books include biographies of U.S. presidents and their wives, biographies of people working in our neighborhoods, phonics books for beginning readers, and informational books about birds and Native Americans. Alice K. Flanagan lives in Chicago, Illinois.

Svetlana Zhurkina was born and grew up in Russia. As a child she was fascinated by picture books, especially fairy tales and folktales. She liked to draw and paint illustrations for her favorite stories. Reading and painting are still her favorite hobbies. Svetlana lives in Mankato, Minnesota, with her husband Dimitri, their daughter Katia, and a tabby cat Tishka. This is her first illustrated book.